Included

Written by Megan Prendergast Illustrated by Alexander Johnson

MM&C, LLC.

ISBN 978-0-578-54981-1

For Calum, my little love. May you always be kind, know you are loved, and feel included.

For my furry loves, Waylon and June, who only know unconditional love and always want to feel included.

For Marc, my first love. For being right by my side as we go through this crazy journey called life.

For my parents and grandparents. For teaching me to always be kind, to be accepting of everyone, and to help everyone feel included.

I love you all,
Megan

Sometimes other kids may
seem **different** to you,
but that does not make them
any less special than you.

Some may be bigger,
some may be smaller,
but it does not matter
who is taller.

Some may use a wheelchair
that goes round and round,
some may need crutches
to get around town.

Some may have glasses to help them see,
some may use hearing aids
to hear you and me.

Some may need more time
or help around,
some may not like bright lights
or loud sounds.

Some kids may have lots of hair, but other kids' heads may be bare.

When someone seems different than you, remember that they are the same, too. What really matters is not something you can see with your eyes, what matters most is actually inside.

What matters the most is being kind, no matter what differences the outside may find. On the inside you may be surprised to see that this person likes the same things as me!

You are all so very **special** and **loved**, by all of your family and friends given from above.

So when you see a kid that you may not know, remember to **be kind** and go say, "Hello!" At the end of the day, we all want to be **Included.**